STAND UP, MR DICKENS

MR DICKENS

A DICKENS ANTHOLOGY

Stand Up, Mr Dickens

A Dickens Anthology

Presented by EDWARD BLISHEN
Illustrated by JILL BENNETT

HOUGHTON MIFFLIN COMPANY
Boston New York 1996

First American edition 1996 published by Houghton Mifflin Company

First published in Great Britain in 1995 by Orion Children's Books,
a division of the Orion Publishing Group Ltd.

For information about this and other Houghton Mifflin trade and reference books
and multimedia products, visit The Bookstore at Houghton Mifflin on the
World Wide Web at (http://www.hmco.com/trade/).

Manufactured in Italy

The text of this book is set in 11-point Sabon.
The illustrations are watercolor, crayon, and pen and ink.

10 9 8 7 6 5 4 3 2 1

Library of Congress Cataloging-in-Publication Data
Blishen, Edward
Stand up, Mr. Dickens : a Dickens anthology / presented by Edward Blishen :
illustrated by Jill Bennett. — 1st American ed.
p.   cm.
Summary: Portrays the life of the famed English novelist and describes how he
entertained audiences by reading his stories aloud. Includes excerpts from "The
Pickwick Papers," "Oliver Twist," "A Christmas Carol," "Dombey and Son,"
"David Copperfield," and "Great Expectations."
ISBN 0-395-75656-1
1. Dickens, Charles, 1812-1870—Biography—Juvenile literature. 2. Dickens,
Charles, 1812-1870—Knowledge—Performing arts—Juvenile literature.
3. Novelists, English—19th century—Biography—Juvenile literature. 4. Oral
reading—History—19th century—Juvenile literature. [1. Dickens, Charles,
1812-1870. 2. Authors, English. 3. English literature.] I. Bennett, Jill, ill.
II. Dickens, Charles, 1812-1870. Novels. Selections. III. Title.
PR4581.B55   1996   823'.8—dc20   [B]   95-18237   CIP   AC

To
Marilyn Malin,
Rodney and Nancy
for all their help
and advice

CONTENTS

STAND UP, MR DICKENS

Imagine a platform, gaslit. There's a reading desk, which will be level with the waist of the reader when shortly he appears and sits at it. There are ledges on each side: one holds a jug of water and a glass, and the other at the moment is empty. There's an oblong of wood on the desk. The hall is full: there is excitement in the air.

But then there are never empty seats at these readings. When one of the most famous men in the world reads from his books (he is, someone has said, the greatest reader of the greatest writer of the age), there are more people who want tickets than there are tickets.

Now the gaslight is turned up, so that it's quite fiercely bright. This great brightness by the desk, and elsewhere, shadows and darkness. And now he has stepped on to the platform. I won't waste words on his appearance; the picture will show you how he looks. Notice particularly the gold watch chain. (He loves jewellery, and colourful waistcoats.) He gazes hard at the audience. They said that everybody at a reading, every single man and woman, felt he looked at him or her directly. When he was reading in America once, someone said the whole audience became one eyeball! It is very important to him that he gathers the audience in – captures them – with his eyes (which are wonderfully expressive). Now on that empty ledge he places his gloves and a handkerchief. The reading is about to begin.

He was a *marvellous* reader. It wasn't just that he had a voice for each character. (Though he did.) It wasn't just that he had a face for each character. (But he had.) It wasn't just what he did with his hands. He rubbed them and patted them; he flourished all his fingers; he shook them, he pointed them, he turned them (his fingers) into a whole company of actors. When in a reading from *A Christmas Carol* he came to an evening at the Fezziwigs, a happy

Christmas scene full of music and dancing, each finger became a leg of one of the Fezziwig family. And when, reading from *David Copperfield*, he had one character slapping another on the shoulder, they said you could feel the slap, and your own shoulder stung a little . . . In the same novel there's a tremendous storm scene, and once when he was reading that passage and describing an immense wave that was rearing into the black screaming air, ready to come crashing down, tons of terrifying water, someone in the audience cried out in alarm, seeming to *see* the wave, afraid the reader might be swept away . . .

But it wasn't just these marvels that held the audience spellbound. It was the stories themselves.

The story of Charles Dickens the man was astonishing – he was the most famous novelist in England when he was still in his early twenties – and *that* story, all his experiences, fed the brimming, heartbreaking, wonderfully funny, frightening, heartwarming stories that formed his great sequence of novels, up to

the last, which he never finished, dying when he was in the middle of writing it –
the for ever unsolved *Mystery of Edwin Drood* . . .

You wondered about that oblong block of wood on the desk? You see, now
he's ready to begin, how he leans his elbow on it! It gives him much-needed
support in a reading that usually spreads over two hours, with an interval, and
for which he'd prepare with something like two hundred rehearsals.

And now Dickens opens the book he is carrying. He is about to read from the
first novel in that great sequence: *The Pickwick Papers.*

IF YOU'D MET DICKENS in April 1836, you'd have made the acquaintance of a not particularly important-seeming young man who was working as a shorthand reporter in the House of Commons, and had just published a collection of comic sketches he'd written for magazines. (He always loved odd names; and the name he gave himself when he wrote those sketches was Boz.)

But if you'd waited to meet him until the end of the same year, you'd have found yourself in the company of a 24-year-old who'd become, as he was to remain, one of the most famous men in Britain. What had happened in between was that he'd written *The Pickwick Papers*.

It began with a publisher, and an idea the publisher had. In those days there was a fashion for books in which the most important part was played by the illustrations. The publisher's idea was for a book of this kind – there was to be a club of Cockney sportsmen, who'd go out into the country shooting and fishing and so on, and, not being very good at these things, get into comic trouble. He had an illustrator in mind: all he wanted was someone who would take his cue from the illustrations and write the text. The publisher had admired *Sketches by Boz*, and he thought Dickens might be his man. And – quite wonderfully – Dickens was. But not at all in the way the publisher, or the illustrator, had imagined. Dickens wasn't going to provide words to match pictures already drawn. With him, the words came first.

In the end, nobody (except the illustrator) complained, partly because Dickens was an extraordinarily strong-minded young man, but mostly because the words were so marvellous. And the

4

characters created by those words were marvellous too. There were, best of all, Mr Samuel Pickwick, round and jolly and decent, and his manservant, Sam Weller, lively and quick-witted and utterly to be depended upon. There were the members of the Pickwick Club – Augustus Snodgrass, Tracy Tupman and Nathaniel Winkle. There was Alfred Jingle, who talked like no one else (actually like a telegram) and wasn't to be trusted. There was Mr Pickwick's landlady, Mrs Bardell, who nearly ruined him; and there was the fat boy, who made everybody's flesh creep. And there were scores of others.

Pickwick was published in monthly instalments at a shilling a copy. Of the first number the publisher printed four hundred copies; long before he got to the end, twenty months later, he was printing forty thousand copies – a hundred times as many. By then there were cigars and hats and coats named after Pickwick, and hundreds of people had called their dogs and cats Sam. 'All the boys and girls talk his fun,' someone said, meaning that they set out to talk like Sam Weller, or Mr Jingle. A man who was dying, and was not otherwise to be comforted, was reported to have said, 'Well, thank God, *Pickwick* will be out in ten days, anyway.'

The Pickwick Papers isn't so much a story as a beautiful tangle of stories. All you need to know in order to enjoy this adventure (or misadventure) of the members of the Pickwick Club is that they are spending Christmas with a hospitable friend, old Wardle, at his home, Manor Farm, Dingley Dell. Also present are two lively young medical students, Benjamin Allen and Bob Sawyer, and a number of ladies, including the three Misses Wardle, Emily, Isabella and Rachael, and Miss Arabella Allen.

'Now,' said Wardle, 'what say you to an hour on the ice? We shall have plenty of time.'

'Capital!' said Mr Benjamin Allen.

'Prime!' ejaculated Mr Bob Sawyer.

'You skate, of course, Winkle?' said Wardle.

'Ye-yes; oh, yes,' replied Mr Winkle. 'I – I – am *rather* out of practice.'

'Oh, *do* skate, Mr Winkle,' said Arabella. 'I like to see it so much.'

'Oh, it is *so* graceful,' said another young lady.

A third young lady said it was elegant, and a fourth expressed her opinion that it was 'swan-like'.

'I should be very happy, I'm sure,' said Mr Winkle, reddening; 'but I have no skates.'

This objection was at once overruled. Trundle had a couple of pairs, and the fat boy announced that there were half a dozen more downstairs: whereat Mr Winkle expressed exquisite delight, and looked exquisitely uncomfortable.

Old Wardle led the way to a pretty large sheet of ice; and the fat boy and Mr Weller having swept away the snow which had fallen on it during the night, Mr Bob Swayer adjusted his skates with a dexterity which to Mr Winkle was perfectly marvellous, and described circles with his left leg, and cut figures of eight, without once stopping for breath, to the excessive satisfaction of old Mr Pickwick, Mr Tupman, and the ladies: which reached a pitch of positive enthusiasm, when old Wardle and Benjamin Allen, assisted by the aforesaid Bob Sawyer, performed some mystic evolutions, which they called a reel.

All this time, Mr Winkle, with his face and hands blue with the cold, had been forcing a gimlet into the soles of his feet, and putting his skates on, with the points behind, and getting the straps into a very complicated and entangled state, with the assistance of Mr Snodgrass, who knew rather less about skates than a Hindoo. At length, however, with the assistance of Mr Weller, the unfortunate skates were firmly screwed and buckled on, and Mr Winkle was raised to his feet.

'Now, then, sir,' said Sam, in an encouraging tone; 'off vith you, and show 'em how to do it.'

'Stop, Sam, stop!' said Mr Winkle, trembling violently, and clutching hold of Sam's arms with the grasp of a drowning man. 'How slippery it is, Sam!'

'Not an uncommon thing upon ice, sir,' replied Mr Weller. 'Hold up, sir!'

This last observation of Mr Weller's bore reference to a demonstration Mr Winkle made at the instant, of a frantic desire to throw his feet in the air, and dash the back of his head on the ice.

'These – these – are very awkward skates; ain't they, Sam?' inquired Mr Winkle, staggering.

'I'm afeerd there's a orkard gen'l'm'n in 'em, sir,' replied Sam.

'Now, Winkle,' cried Mr Pickwick, quite unconscious that there was anything the matter. 'Come; the ladies are all anxiety.'

'Yes, yes,' replied Mr Winkle, with a ghastly smile. 'I'm coming.'

'Just a goin' to begin,' said Sam, endeavouring to disengage himself. 'Now, sir, start off!'

'Stop an instant, Sam,' gasped Mr Winkle, clinging most affectionately to Mr Weller. 'I find I've got a couple of coats at home that I don't want, Sam. You may have them, Sam.'

'Thank'ee, sir,' replied Mr Weller.

'Never mind touching your hat, Sam,' said Mr Winkle, hastily. 'You needn't take your hand away to do that. I meant to have given you five shillings this morning for a Christmas-box, Sam. I'll give it you this afternoon, Sam.'

'You're very good, sir,' replied Mr Weller.

'Just hold me at first, Sam; will you?' said Mr Winkle. 'There – that's right. I shall soon get in the way of it, Sam. Not too fast, Sam; not too fast.'

Mr Winkle stooping forward, with his body half doubled up, was being assisted over the ice by Mr Weller, in a very singular and un-swan-like manner, when Mr Pickwick most innocently shouted from the opposite bank:

'Sam!'

'Sir?'

'Here. I want you.'

'Let go, sir,' said Sam. 'Don't you hear the governor a callin'? Let go, sir.'

With a violent effort, Mr Weller disengaged himself from the grasp of the agonized Pickwickian, and, in so doing, administered a considerable impetus to the unhappy Mr Winkle; and that unfortunate gentleman bore swiftly down into the centre of the reel, at the very moment when Mr Bob Sawyer was performing a flourish of unparalleled beauty. Mr Winkle struck wildly against him, and with a loud crash they both fell heavily down.

Mr Pickwick ran to the spot. Bob Sawyer had risen to his feet, but Mr Winkle was far too wise to do anything of the kind, in skates.

'Are you hurt?' Inquired Mr Benjamin Allen, with great anxiety.

'Not much,' said Mr Winkle, rubbing

his back very hard.

Mr Pickwick was excited and indignant. He beckoned to Mr Weller, and said in a stern voice, 'Take his skates off.'

'No; but really I had scarcely begun,' remonstrated Mr Winkle.

'Take his skates off,' repeated Mr Pickwick firmly.

The command was not to be resisted. Mr Winkle allowed Sam to obey it in silence.

'Lift him up,' said Mr Pickwick. Sam assisted him to rise.

Mr Pickwick retired a few paces apart from the bystanders; and, beckoning his friend to approach, fixed a searching look upon him, and uttered in a low, but distinct and emphatic tone, these remarkable words:

'You're a humbug, sir.'

'A what?' said Mr Winkle, starting.

'A humbug, sir. I will speak plainer, if you wish. An impostor, sir.'

With those words, Mr Pickwick turned slowly on his heel, and rejoined his friends.

Meanwhile Mr Weller and the fat boy, having cut out a slide, were exercising themselves thereupon, in a very masterly and brilliant manner. Sam Weller, in particular, was displaying that beautiful feat of fancy-sliding which is known as 'knocking at the cobbler's door', and which is achieved by skimming over the ice on one foot, and occasionally giving a postman's knock upon it with the other. It was a good long slide, and there was something in the motion which Mr Pickwick, who was very cold with standing still, could not help envying.

'It looks a nice warm exercise that, doesn't it?' he inquired of Wardle.

'Ah, it does indeed,' replied Wardle. 'Do you slide?'

'I used to do so, when I was a boy,' replied Mr Pickwick.

'Try it now,' said Wardle.

'Oh do please, Mr Pickwick!' cried all the ladies.

'I should be very happy to afford you any amusement,' replied Mr Pickwick, 'but I haven't done such a thing these thirty years.'

'Pooh, pooh! Nonsense!' said Wardle, dragging off his skates. 'Here; I'll keep you company; come along!' And away went the good-tempered old fellow down the slide, with a rapidity which came very close upon Mr Weller, and beat the fat boy all to nothing.

Mr Pickwick paused, considered, pulling off his gloves and put them in his hat; took two or three short runs, stopped short as often, and at last took another run, and went slowly and gravely down the slide, with his feet about a yard and a quarter apart, amidst the gratified shouts of all the spectators.

'Keep the pot a bilin', sir!' said Sam; and down went Wardle again, and then Mr Pickwick, and then Sam, and then Mr Winkle, and then Mr Bob Sawyer, and then the fat boy, and then Mr Snodgrass, following closely upon each other's heels, and running after each other with as much eagerness as if all their future prospects in life depended on it.

The sport was at its height, the sliding was at the quickest, the laughter was at the loudest, when a sharp smart crack was heard. There was a quick rush towards the bank, a wild scream from the ladies, and a shout from Mr Tupman. A large mass of ice disappeared; the water bubbled up over it; Mr Pickwick's hat, gloves, and handkerchief were floating on the surface; and this was all of Mr Pickwick that anybody could see.

Dismay and anguish were depicted on every countenance, the males turned pale, and the females fainted, Mr Snodgrass and Mr Winkle grasped each other by the hand, and gazed at the spot where their leader had gone down: while Mr Tupman, by way of rendering the promptest assistance, and at the same time conveying to any persons who might be within hearing the clearest possible notion of the catastrophe, ran off across the country at his utmost speed, screaming 'Fire!' with all his might.

It was at this moment that a face, head, and shoulders emerged from beneath the water, and disclosed the features and spectacles of Mr Pickwick.

'Keep yourself up for an instant – for only one instant!' bawled Mr Snodgrass.

'Yes, do; let me implore you – for my sake!' roared Mr Winkle, rather unnecessarily; the probability being that if Mr Pickwick had declined to keep himself up for anybody else's sake, it would have occurred to him that he might as well do so, for his own.

'Do you feel the bottom there, old fellow?' said Wardle.

'Yes, certainly,' replied Mr Pickwick, wringing the water from his head and face, and gasping for breath. The fears of the spectators having been further relieved by the fat boy's suddenly recollecting that the water was nowhere more than five feet deep, prodigies of valour were performed to get him out. After a vast quantity of splashing, and cracking, and struggling, Mr Pickwick once more stood on dry land.

'Oh, he'll catch his death of cold,' said Emily.

'Dear old thing!' said Arabella. 'Let me wrap this shawl round you, Mr Pickwick.'

'Ah, that's the best thing you can do,' said Wardle; 'and when you've got it on, run home as fast as your legs can carry you, and jump into bed directly.'

A dozen shawls were offered on the instant. Three or four of the thickest having been selected, Mr Pickwick was wrapped up, and started off, under the guidance of Mr Weller: presenting the singular phenomenon of an elderly gentleman, dripping wet, and without a hat, with his arms bound down to his sides, skimming over the ground, without any clearly defined purpose, at the rate of six good English miles an hour.

WHAT SHOULD THIS suddenly famous young man do next? Well, he got married, and he became the editor of a magazine. And for this magazine he wrote *Oliver Twist* – again in monthly instalments. When he started on it, he hadn't finished *The Pickwick Papers*. But doing more than one thing at once came naturally to Dickens.

You could say that when he wrote *Oliver Twist* he had two special thoughts in his busy head. We'll fully understand the first of these when we come to *David Copperfield*. There was a reason why he was always drawn to the story of a boy who seems to have the whole world against him, and to have little hope of happiness. Oliver begins as just such a boy. Dickens also wanted to make people aware of something that made him furiously angry. There'd been a new law passed – the new Poor Law. To save money, the workhouses, where the jobless and penniless were lodged, were to be made so unpleasant that even these desperate people would shrink from them, part of the unpleasantness being that the food provided would be as scanty and disagreeable as possible. Some of the wonderful energy with which Dickens wrote always came from his wish to draw attention to such cruelties and injustices.

But starting in a workhouse, with Oliver as a helpless orphan, *Oliver Twist* becomes a tremendous story, spreading itself into the slums of London (where Oliver is involved, despite himself, with thieves, some as young as he is) and into more comfortable places, as Oliver's fortunes rise. Those fortunes rise, and fall, and rise again, while we hold our breath, till the very end of the novel. There's a character, Bill Sikes, and a murder he commits, and a manhunt that follows, ending among the rooftops of London, which provided Dickens with one of his most extraordinary readings. Having read it for the first time to specially chosen guests, he noted gleefully that they were all 'unmistakably pale, and had horror-struck faces'.

The story so far . . . A young woman, who has been found lying in the street, her shoes worn to pieces by walking, is taken to the workhouse, where she gives birth to a baby boy, and dies. The naming of children in such circumstances is left, in this workhouse, to the beadle, Mr Bumble. (A beadle was a parish officer who kept order in church, punished people who broke the law in small ways, and so on.) Mr Bumble chooses names in alphabetical order: it's time for T, and the baby is named Oliver Twist. At nine, with other workhouse boys, he's set to work, picking oakum (cruelly painful and boring labour, picking old rope to pieces). For food they have little more than three bowls of gruel, a very thin porridge, a day.

OLIVER TWIST

THE ROOM IN WHICH the boys were fed was a large stone hall, with a copper at one end: out of which the master, dressed in an apron for the purpose, and assisted by one or two women, ladled the gruel at meal-times. Of this each boy had one porringer, and no more – except on occasions of great public rejoicing, when he had two ounces and a quarter of bread besides. The bowls never wanted washing. The boys polished them with their spoons till they shone again; and when they had performed this operation (which never took very long, the spoons being nearly as large as the bowls), they would sit staring at the copper, with such eager eyes, as if they could have devoured the very bricks of which it was composed; employing themselves, meanwhile, in sucking their fingers, with the view of catching up any stray splashes of gruel that might have been cast thereon. Boys have generally excellent appetites. Oliver Twist and his companions suffered the tortures of slow starvation for three months. At last they got so wild with hunger that one boy, who was tall for his age, and hadn't been used to that sort of thing (for his father had kept a small cook's shop), hinted darkly to his companions that unless he had another basin of gruel every day, he was afraid he might some night happen to eat the boy who slept next him, who happened to be a weakly youth of tender age. He had a wild, hungry eye; and they believed him. A council was held; lots were cast who should walk up to the master after supper that evening, and ask for more; and it fell to Oliver Twist.

The evening arrived; the boys took their places. The master, in his cook's uniform, stationed himself at the copper; his assistants ranged themselves behind him; the gruel

was served out; and a long grace was said. The gruel disappeared; the boys whispered to each other, and winked at Oliver; while his next neighbours nudged him. Child as he was, he was desperate with hunger, and reckless with misery. He rose from the table; and advancing to the master, basin and spoon in hand, said:

'Please, sir, I want some more.'

The master was a fat, healthy man; but he turned very pale. He gazed in stupefied astonishment on the small rebel for some seconds, and then clung for support to the copper. The assistants were paralysed with wonder; the boys with fear.

'What!' said the master at length, in a faint voice.

'Please, sir,' replied Oliver, 'I want some more.'

The master aimed a blow at Oliver's head with the ladle; pinioned him in his arms; and shrieked aloud for the beadle.

The board of the workhouse were sitting in solemn conclave, when Mr Bumble rushed into the room in great excitement, and addressing the gentleman in the high chair, said,

'Mr Limbkins, I beg your pardon, sir! Oliver Twist has asked for more!'

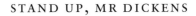

There was a general start. Horror was depicted on every countenance.

'For *more*!' said Mr Limbkins. 'Compose yourself, Bumble, and answer me distinctly. Do I understand that he asked for more, after he had eaten the supper allotted by the dietary?'

'He did, sir,' replied Bumble.

'That boy will be hung,' said a gentleman in a white waistcoat. 'I know that boy will be hung.'

Oliver was ordered into instant confinement; and a bill was next morning pasted on the outside of the gate, offering a reward of five pounds to anybody who would take Oliver Twist off the hands of the parish. In other words, five pounds and Oliver Twist were offered to any man or woman who wanted an apprentice to any trade, business, or calling.

'I never was more convinced of anything in my life,' said the gentleman in the white waistcoat, as he knocked at the gate and read the bill next morning: 'I never was more convinced of anything in my life, than I am that that boy will come to be hung.'

For a week afterwards, Oliver remained a close prisoner in the dark and solitary room to which he had been consigned by the wisdom and mercy of the board. He cried bitterly all day; and, when the long, dismal night came on, spread his little hands before his eyes to shut out the darkness, and crouching in the corner, tried to sleep: ever and anon waking with a start and tremble, and drawing himself closer and closer to the wall, as if to feel even its cold hard surface were a protection in the gloom and loneliness which surrounded him.

Let it not be supposed that, during the period of his solitary incarceration, Oliver was denied the benefit of exercise, or the pleasure of society. It was nice cold weather, and he was allowed to perform his ablutions every morning under the pump, in a stone yard, in the presence of Mr Bumble, who prevented his catching cold, and caused a tingling sensation to pervade his frame, by repeated applications of the cane. As for society, he was carried every other day into the hall where the boys dined, and there sociably flogged as a public warning and example.

It chanced one morning, while Oliver's affairs were in this comfortable state, that Mr Gamfield, chimney-sweep, went his way down the High Street, deeply cogitating in his mind his ways and means of paying certain arrears of rent, for which his landlord had become rather pressing. He was alternately cudgelling his brains and his donkey, when, passing the workhouse, his eyes encountered the bill on the gate.

'Wo-o!' said Mr Gamfield to the donkey.

The donkey was in a state of profound abstraction: wondering, probably, whether he was destined to be regaled with a cabbage-stalk or two when he had disposed of the two sacks of soot with which the little cart was laden; so, without noticing the word of command, he jogged onward.

Mr Gamfield ran after the donkey, caught hold of the bridle, and gave his jaw a sharp wrench, by way of gentle reminder that he was not his own master; and by these means turned him round. He then gave him a blow on the head, just to stun him till he came back again. Having completed these arrangements, he walked up to the gate to read the bill.

The gentleman with the white waistcoat was standing at the gate with his hands behind him. Having witnessed the little dispute between Mr Gamfield and the donkey, he smiled joyously when that person came up to read the bill, for he saw at once that Mr Gamfield was exactly the sort of master Oliver Twist wanted. Mr Gamfield smiled, too, as he perused the document; for five pounds was just the sum he had been wishing for. So, he spelt the bill through again, from beginning to end; and then, touching his fur cup, accosted the gentleman in the white waistcoat.

'This here boy, sir, wot the parish wants to 'prentis,' said Mr Gamfield.

'Ay, my man,' said the gentleman in the white waistcoat. 'What of him?'

'If the parish vould like him to learn a right pleasant trade, in a good 'spectable chimbley-sweepin' bisness,' said Mr Gamfield, 'I wants a 'prentis, and I am ready to take him.'

'Walk in,' said the gentleman in the white waistcoat. Mr Gamfield having lingered behind to give the donkey another wrench of the jaw, as a caution not to run away in his absence, followed the gentleman with the white waistcoat into the room where Oliver had first seen him.

'It's a nasty trade,' said Mr Limbkins, when Gamfield had again stated his wish.

'Young boys have been smothered in chimneys before now,' said another gentleman.

'That's acause they damped the straw afore they lit it in the chimbley to make 'em come down agin,' said Gamfield; 'that's all smoke, and no blaze; vereas smoke ain't o' no use at all in making a boy come down, for it only sinds him to sleep, and that's wot he likes. Boys is wery obstinit, and wery lazy, gen'lemen, and there's nothink like a good hot blaze to make 'em come down vith a run. It's humane too, gen'lemen, acause, even if they've stuck in the chimbley, roasting their feet makes 'em struggle to hextricate theirselves.'

The gentleman in the white waistcoat appeared very much amused by this explanation; but his mirth was speedily checked by a look from Mr Limbkins.

The board then proceeded to converse among themselves for a few minutes. When their whispering ceased, and the members of the board had resumed their seats and their solemnity, Mr Limbkins said:

'We have considered your proposition, and we don't approve of it.'

'Not at all,' said the gentleman in the white waistcoat.

'Decidedly not,' added the other members.

As it did happen to be rumoured that Mr Gamfield had bruised three or four boys to death already, it occurred to him that the board had, perhaps, in some unaccountable freak, taken it into their heads that this ought to influence their proceedings. It was very unlike their general mode of doing business, if they had; but still, as he had no particular wish to revive the rumour, he twisted his cap in his hands, and walked slowly from the table.

'So you won't let me have him, gen'lemen?' said Mr Gamfield, pausing near the door.

'No,' replied Mr Limbkins; 'at least, as it's a nasty business, we think you ought to take something less than the premium we offered.'

Mr Gamfield's countenance brightened, as, with a quick step, he returned to the table, and said,

'What'll you give, gen'lemen? Come! Don't be too hard on a poor man. What'll you give?'

'I should say three pound ten was plenty,' said Mr Limbkins.

'Ten shillings too much,' said the gentleman in the white waistcoat.

'Come!' said Gamfield. 'Say four pound, gen'lemen. Say four pound, and you've got rid on him for good and all. There!'

'Three pound ten,' repeated Mr Limbkins, firmly.

'Come! I'll split the difference, gen'lemen,' urged Gamfield.

'Not a farthing more,' was the firm reply of Mr Limbkins.

'You're desperate hard upon me, gen'lemen,' said Gamfield, wavering.

'Pooh, pooh! Nonsense!' said the gentleman in the white waistcoat. 'He'd be

cheap with nothing at all as a premium. Take him, you silly fellow! He's just the boy for you. He wants the stick, now and then: it'll do him good; and his board needn't come very expensive, for he hasn't been overfed since he was born. Ha! ha! ha!'

Mr Gamfield gave a look at the faces round the table, and, observing a smile on all of them, gradually broke into a smile himself. The bargain was made. Mr Bumble was at once instructed that Oliver Twist and his indentures were to be conveyed before the magistrate, for signature and approval, that very afternoon.

So little Oliver, to his astonishment, was released from bondage, and ordered to put himself into a clean shirt. He had hardly achieved this very unusual performance, when Mr Bumble brought him, with his own hands, a basin of gruel, and the holiday allowance of two ounces and a quarter of bread. At this tremendous sight, Oliver began to cry very piteously: thinking, not unnaturally, that the board must have determined to kill him for some useful purpose, or they never would have begun to fatten him up in that way.

'Don't make your eyes red, Oliver, but eat your food and be thankful,' said Mr Bumble. 'You're a going to be made a 'prentice of, Oliver.'

'A 'prentice, sir!' said the child, trembling.

'Yes, Oliver,' said Mr Bumble. 'The kind and blessed gentlemen which is so many parents to you, Oliver, when you have none of your own, are a going to 'prentice you; and to set you up in life, and make a man of you; although the expense to the parish is three pound ten! – three pound ten, Oliver! – seventy shillins – one hundred and forty sixpences! – and all for a naughty orphan which nobody can't love.'

As Mr Bumble paused to take breath, after delivering this address in an awful voice, the tears rolled down the poor child's face, and he sobbed bitterly.

'Come,' said Mr Bumble, 'come, Oliver! Wipe your eyes with the cuffs of your jacket, and don't cry into your gruel; that's a very foolish action, Oliver.' It certainly was, for there was quite enough water in it already.

On their way to the magistrate, Mr Bumble instructed Oliver that all he would have to do would be to look very happy, and say, when the gentleman asked him if he wanted to be apprenticed, that he should like it very much indeed; both of which injunctions Oliver promised to obey: the rather as Mr Bumble threw in a gentle hint that if he failed in either particular, there was no telling what would be done to him. When they arrived at the office, he was shut up in a little room by himself, and admonished by Mr Bumble to stay there, until he came back to fetch him.

There the boy remained, with a palpitating heart, for half an hour. At the end of which time Mr Bumble thrust in his head and said aloud:

'Now, Oliver, my dear, come to the gentleman.' As Mr Bumble said this, he put on a grim and threatening look, and added, in a low voice, 'Mind what I told you, you young rascal!'

And Oliver was led at once into an adjoining room, the door of which was open. It was a large room, with a great window. Behind a desk sat two old gentlemen with powdered heads: one of whom was reading the newspaper; while the other was perusing, with the aid of a pair of tortoiseshell spectacles, a small piece of parchment which lay before him. Mr Limbkins was standing in front of the desk on one side; and Mr Gamfield, with a partially washed face, on the other; while two or three bluff-looking men, in top-boots, were lounging about.

The old gentleman with the spectacles gradually dozed off, over the little bit of parchment; and there was a short pause, after Oliver had been stationed by Mr Bumble in front of the desk.

'This is the boy, your worship,' said Mr Bumble.

The old gentleman who was reading the newspaper raised his head for a moment, and pulled the other old gentleman by the sleeve; whereupon the last-mentioned old gentleman woke up.

'Oh, is this the boy?' said the old gentleman.

'This is him, sir,' replied Mr Bumble. 'Bow to the magistrate, my dear.'

'Well,' said the old gentleman, 'I suppose he's fond of chimney-sweeping?'

'He dotes on it, your worship,' replied Bumble, giving Oliver a sly pinch to intimate that he had better not say he didn't.

'And he *will* be a sweep, will he?' inquired the old gentleman.

'If we was to bind him to any other trade tomorrow, he'd run away simultaneous, your worship,' replied Bumble.

'And this man that's to be his master – you, sir – you'll treat him well, and feed him, and do all that sort of thing, will you?' said the old gentleman.

'When I says I will, I means I will,' replied Mr Gamfield doggedly.

'You're a rough speaker, my friend, but you look an honest, open-hearted man,' said the old gentleman, turning his spectacles in the direction of Mr Gamfield, whose villainous countenance was a regular stamped receipt for cruelty. But the magistrate was half blind and half childish, so he couldn't reasonably be expected to discern what other people did.

'I hope I am, sir,' said Mr Gamfield, with an ugly leer.

'I have no doubt you are, my friend,' replied the old gentleman, fixing his spectacles more firmly on his nose, and looking about him for the inkstand.

It was the critical moment of Oliver's fate. If the inkstand had been where the old gentleman thought it was, he would have dipped his pen into it, and signed the indentures, and Oliver would have been straightway hurried off. But, as it chanced to be immediately under his nose, it followed, as a matter of course, that he looked all over his desk for it, without finding it; and happening in the course of his search to look straight before him, his gaze encountered the pale and terrified face of Oliver Twist, who, despite all Bumble's pinches, was regarding the repulsive countenance of his future master with a mingled expression of horror and fear, too palpable to be mistaken, even by a half-blind magistrate.

The old gentleman stopped, laid down his pen, and looked from Oliver to Mr Limbkins, who attempted to take snuff with a cheerful and unconcerned aspect.

'My boy!' said the old gentleman. 'You look pale and alarmed. What is the matter?'

'Stand a little away from him, Beadle,' said the other magistrate, laying aside the paper, and leaning forward with an expression of interest. 'Now, boy, tell us what's the matter; don't be afraid.'

Oliver fell on his knees, and clasping his hands together, prayed that they would order him back to the dark room – that they would starve him – kill him if they pleased – rather than send him away with that dreadful man.

'Well!' said Mr Bumble, raising his hands and his eyes with most impressive solemnity. 'Well, of all the artful and designing orphans that ever I see, Oliver, you are one of the most barefacedest!'

'Hold your tongue, Beadle,' said the second old gentleman.

'I beg your worship's pardon,' said Mr Bumble. 'Did your worship speak to me?'

'Yes. Hold your tongue.'

Mr Bumble was stupefied with astonishment. A beadle ordered to hold his tongue!

The old gentleman in the tortoiseshell spectacles looked at his companion; he nodded.

'We refuse to sanction these indentures,' said the old gentleman, tossing aside the piece of parchment as he spoke.

'I hope,' stammered Mr Limbkins – 'I hope the magistrates will not form the opinion that the authorities have been guilty of any improper conduct, on the unsupported testimony of a mere child.'

'The magistrates are not called upon to pronounce any opinion on the matter,' said the second old gentleman sharply. 'Take the boy back to the workhouse, and treat him kindly. He seems to want it.'

That same evening, the gentleman in the white waistcoat most positively and decidedly affirmed, not only that Oliver would be hung, but that he would be drawn and quartered into the bargain. Mr Bumble shook his head with gloomy mystery, and said he wished he might come to good; whereunto Mr Gamfield replied that he wished he might come to him; which, although he agreed with the beadle in most matters, would seem to be a wish of a totally opposite description.

The next morning, the public were once more informed that Oliver Twist was again To Let, and that five pounds would be paid to anybody who would take possession of him.

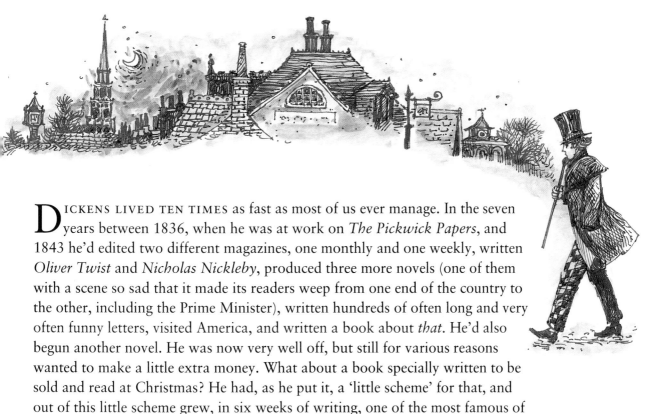

DICKENS LIVED TEN TIMES as fast as most of us ever manage. In the seven years between 1836, when he was at work on *The Pickwick Papers*, and 1843 he'd edited two different magazines, one monthly and one weekly, written *Oliver Twist* and *Nicholas Nickleby*, produced three more novels (one of them with a scene so sad that it made its readers weep from one end of the country to the other, including the Prime Minister), written hundreds of often long and very often funny letters, visited America, and written a book about *that*. He'd also begun another novel. He was now very well off, but still for various reasons wanted to make a little extra money. What about a book specially written to be sold and read at Christmas? He had, as he put it, a 'little scheme' for that, and out of this little scheme grew, in six weeks of writing, one of the most famous of all books. He called it *A Christmas Carol*.

In a letter he told a friend that he'd been 'so closely occupied with my little Carol that I never left home before the owls went out'. And when the owls did emerge for their nightly hunt, Dickens too would emerge from his house and set out on one of his great walks through London, thinking out the next steps in the story.

Reading from *A Christmas Carol* (always including the ghostly passage that follows, with which he chilled the blood of thousands of listeners both in Britain

and in America) gave him special pleasure. He would invite his audiences to imagine they were seated round a Christmas fire; they were to laugh and cry as they wished – that would be no disturbance to him, but a delight. He *needed* his audience. When Queen Victoria said she would like to hear him read from *A Christmas Carol*, meaning she'd like him to come to the palace and read it to her alone, he respectfully suggested that she might find it better to listen to him whilst sitting among others. In these readings he impersonated twenty-three different characters, every one of them (they said) perfectly different from every other.

A Christmas Carol is the story of Ebenezer Scrooge, a miserly man, 'squeezing, wrenching, grasping, scraping, clutching, covetous'. It opens in his office, on Christmas Eve; it's ice-cold in there, for he's too mean to have anything but a very small fire. His clerk's fire is even smaller. Grudgingly he agrees that the clerk should have Christmas Day free to spend with his family. His nephew appears to wish him a happy Christmas. 'Bah!' says Scrooge. 'Humbug!' Two men arrive to ask him to make a small donation to provide comforts for the poor. 'Are there no prisons?' growls Scrooge, refusing.

And then he sets off home . . .

A CHRISTMAS CAROL

SCROOGE TOOK HIS MELANCHOLY dinner in his usual melancholy tavern, and went home to bed. He lived in a gloomy suite of rooms, in a lowering pile of building up a yard, where it had so little business to be that one could scarcely help fancying it must have run there when it was a young house, playing at hide-and-seek with other houses, and have forgotten the way out again. It was old enough now, and dreary enough, for nobody lived in it but Scrooge, the other rooms being all let out as offices. The yard was so dark that even Scrooge, who knew its every stone, was fain to grope with his hands.

Now, it is a fact that there was nothing at all particular about the knocker on the door, except that it was very large. It is also a fact that Scrooge had seen it, night and morning, during his whole residence in that place. Let it also be borne in mind that Scrooge had not bestowed one thought on Marley, since his last mention of his seven-years' dead partner that afternoon. And then let any man explain to me, if he can, how it happened that Scrooge, having his key in the lock of the door, saw in the knocker: not a knocker, but Marley's face.

Marley's face. It was not in shadow as the other objects in the yard were, but had a dismal light about it, like a bad lobster in a dark cellar. It was not angry or ferocious, but looked at Scrooge as Marley used to look: with ghostly spectacles turned up on its ghostly forehead. The hair was curiously stirred, as if by breath or hot air; and, though the eyes were wide open, they were perfectly motionless. That, and its livid colour, made it horrible.

As Scrooge looked fixedly at this phenomenon, it was a knocker again.

To say that he was not startled would be untrue. But he put his hand upon the key he had relinquished, turned it sturdily, walked in, and lighted his candle.

He *did* pause before he shut the door; and he *did* look cautiously behind it first, as if he half expected to be terrified with the sight of Marley's pigtail sticking out into the hall. But there was nothing on the back of the door, except the screws and nuts that held the knocker on; so he said 'Pooh, pooh!' and closed it with a bang.

The sound resounded through the house like thunder. Every room above, and every cask in the wine-merchant's cellars below, appeared to have a separate peel of echoes of its own. Scrooge was not a man to be frightened by echoes. He fastened the door, and walked across the hall, and up the stairs: slowly too: trimming his candle as he went.

You may talk vaguely about driving a coach-and-six up a good old flight of stairs; but I mean to say you might have got a hearse up the staircase, and done it easy. There was plenty of width for that, and room to spare; which is perhaps the reason why Scrooge thought he saw a hearse going on before him in the gloom. Half a dozen gas-lamps out of the street wouldn't have lighted the entry too well, so you may suppose that it was pretty dark with Scrooge's dip.

Up Scrooge went, not caring a bottom for that: darkness is cheap, and Scrooge liked it. But before he shut his heavy door, he walked through his rooms to see that all was right. He had just enough recollection of the face to desire to do that.

Sitting-room, bedroom, lumber-room. All as they should be. Nobody under the table, nobody under the sofa; a small fire in the grate; spoon and basin ready; and the little saucepan of gruel (Scrooge had a cold in his head) upon the hob. Nobody under the bed; nobody in the closet; nobody in his dressing-gown, which was hanging up in a suspicious attitude against the wall. Lumber-room as usual. Old fire-guard, old shoes, two fish-baskets, washing-stand on three legs, and a poker.

Quite satisfied, he closed his door, and locked himself in; double-locked himself in, which was not his custom. Thus secured against surprise, he took off his cravat; put on his dressing-gown and slippers, and his nightcap; and sat down beside the fire to take his gruel.

It was a very low fire indeed; nothing on such a bitter night. He was obliged to sit close to it, and brood over it, before he could extract the least sensation of warmth from such a handful of fuel. The fireplace was an old one, built by some Dutch merchant long ago, and paved all round with quaint Dutch tiles, designed to illustrate the Scriptures. There were Cains and Abels, Pharaohs' daughters, Queens of Sheba, Angelic messengers descending through the air on clouds like feather-beds, Abrahams, Belshazzars, Apostles putting off to sea in butter-boats, hundreds of figures, to attract his thoughts; and yet that face of Marley, seven years dead, came and swallowed up the whole. If each smooth tile had been a blank at first, with power to shape some picture on its surface from the fragments of his thoughts, there would have been a copy of old Marley's head on every one.

'Humbug!' said Scrooge; and walked across the room.

After several turns, he sat down again. As he threw his head back in the chair, his glance happened to rest upon a bell, a disused bell, that hung in the room, and communicated for some purpose now forgotten with a chamber in the highest storey of the building. It was with great astonishment, and with a strange dread, that as he looked, he saw this bell begin to swing. It swung so softly in the outset that it scarcely made a sound; but soon it rang out loudly, and so did every bell in the house.

This might have lasted half a minute, or a minute, but it seemed an hour. The bells ceased as they had begun, together. They were succeeded by a clanking noise, deep down below; as if some person were dragging a heavy chain over the casks in the wine-merchant's cellar. Scrooge then remembered to have heard that ghosts in haunted houses were described as dragging chains.

The cellar-door flew open with a booming sound, and then he heard the noise much louder, on the floors below; then coming up the stairs; then coming straight towards his door.

'It's humbug still!' said Scrooge. 'I won't believe it.'

His colour changed though, when, without a pause, it came on through the heavy door, and passed into the room before his eyes. Upon its coming in, the dying flame leaped up, as though it cried 'I know him! Marley's Ghost!' and fell again.

The same face: the very same. Marley in his pigtail, usual waistcoat, tights and boots; the tassels on the latter bristling, like his pigtail, and his coat-skirts, and the hair upon his head. The chain he drew was clasped about his middle. It was long, and wound about him like a tail; and it was made of cash-boxes, keys, padlocks, ledgers, deeds, and heavy purses wrought in steel. His body was transparent; so that Scrooge, observing him, and looking through his waistcoat, could see the two buttons on his coat behind.

Yet though he looked the phantom through and through, and saw it standing before him; though he felt the chilling influence of its death-cold eyes; and marked the very texture of the folded kerchief bound about its head and chin, which wrapper he had not observed before: he was still incredulous, and fought against his senses.

'How now!' said Scrooge. 'What do you want with me?'

'Much!' – Marley's voice, no doubt about it.

'Who are you?'

'Ask me who I *was*.'

'Who *were* you then?' said Scrooge, raising his voice.

'In life I was your partner, Jacob Marley.'

'Can you – can you sit down?' asked Scrooge, looking doubtfully at him.

'I can.'

'Do it then.'

The Ghost sat down on the opposite side of the fireplace, as if he were quite used to it.

'You don't believe in me,' observed the Ghost.

'I don't,' said Scrooge.

'Why do you doubt your senses?'

'Because,' said Scrooge, 'a little thing affects them. A slight disorder of the stomach makes them cheats. You may be an undigested bit of beef, a blot of mustard, a crumb of cheese, a fragment of underdone potato. There's more of gravy than of grave about you, whatever you are!'

Scrooge was not much in the habit of cracking jokes, nor did he feel, in his heart, by any means waggish then. The truth is that he tried to be smart, as a means of distracting his own attention, and keeping down his terror; for the spectre's voice disturbed the very marrow in his bones.

To sit, staring at those fixed, glazed eyes, in silence for a moment, would play, Scrooge felt, the very deuce with him. There was something very awful, too, in the spectre's being provided with an infernal atmosphere of its own. Scrooge could not feel it himself, but this was clearly the case; for though the Ghost sat perfectly motionless, its hair, and skirts, and tassels were still agitated as by the hot vapour from an oven.

'You see this toothpick?' said Scrooge, returning quickly to the charge; and wishing, though it were only for a second, to divert the vision's stony gaze from himself.

'I do,' replied the Ghost.

'You are not looking at it,' said Scrooge.

'But I see it,' said the Ghost, 'notwithstanding.'

'Well!' returned Scrooge. 'I have but to swallow this, and be for the rest of my days persecuted by a legion of goblins, all of my own creation. Humbug, I tell you – humbug!'

At this the spirit raised a frightful cry, and shook its chain with such a dismal and appalling noise that Scrooge held on tight to his chair, to save himself from falling in a swoon. But how much greater was his horror, when the phantom taking off the bandage round its head, as if it were too warm to wear indoors, its lower jaw dropped down upon its breast!

Scrooge fell upon his knees, and clasped his hands before his face.

'Mercy!' he said. 'Dreadful apparition, why do you trouble me?'

'Man of the worldly mind!' replied the Ghost. 'Do you believe in me or not?'

'I do,' said Scrooge. 'I must. But why do spirits walk the earth, and why do they come to me?'

'It is required of every man,' the Ghost returned, 'that the spirit within him should walk abroad among his fellow-men, and travel far and wide; and if that spirit goes not forth in life, it is condemned to do so after death. It is doomed to wander through the world – oh, woe is me! – and witness what it cannot share, but might have shared on earth, and turned to happiness!'

Again the spectre raised a cry, and shook its chain, and wrung its shadowy hands.

'You are fettered,' said Scrooge, trembling. 'Tell me why.'

'I wear the chain I forged in life,' replied the Ghost. 'I made it link by link, and yard by yard. Is its pattern strange to *you*?'

Scrooge trembled more and more.

'Or would you know,' pursued the Ghost, 'the weight and length of the strong coil you bear yourself? It was full as heavy and as long as this, seven Christmas

Eves ago. You have laboured on it, since. It is a ponderous chain!'

Scrooge glanced about him on the floor, in the expectation of finding himself surrounded by some fifty or sixty fathoms of iron cable: but he could see nothing.

'Jacob,' he said, imploringly. 'Old Jacob Marley, tell me more. Speak comfort to me, Jacob.'

'I have none to give,' the Ghost replied. 'Nor can I tell you what I would. A very little more is all permitted to me. I cannot rest, I cannot stay, I cannot linger anywhere. My spirit never walked beyond our counting-house – mark me! – in life my spirit never roved beyond the narrow limits of our money-changing hole; and weary journeys lie before me!'

'You must have been very slow about it, Jacob,' Scrooge observed.

'Slow!' the Ghost repeated.

'Seven years dead,' mused Scrooge. 'And travelling all the time!'

'The whole time,' said the Ghost. 'No rest, no peace. Incessant torture of remorse.'

'You travel fast?' said Scrooge.

'On the wings of the wind,' replied the Ghost.

'You might have got over a great quantity of ground in seven years,' said Scrooge.

The Ghost, on hearing this, set up another cry, and clanked its chain hideously in the silence of the night.

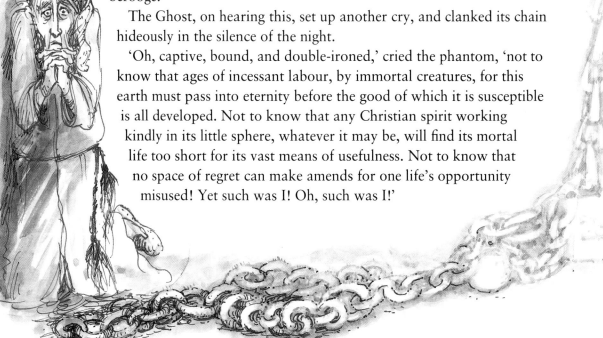

'Oh, captive, bound, and double-ironed,' cried the phantom, 'not to know that ages of incessant labour, by immortal creatures, for this earth must pass into eternity before the good of which it is susceptible is all developed. Not to know that any Christian spirit working kindly in its little sphere, whatever it may be, will find its mortal life too short for its vast means of usefulness. Not to know that no space of regret can make amends for one life's opportunity misused! Yet such was I! Oh, such was I!'

'But you were always a good man of business, Jacob,' faltered Scrooge, who now began to apply this to himself.

'Business!' cried the Ghost, wringing its hands again. 'Mankind was my business. The common welfare was my business; charity, mercy, forbearance, and benevolence were, all, my business. The dealings of my trade were but a drop of water in the comprehensive ocean of my business!'

It held up its chain at arm's length, as if that were the cause of all its unavailing grief, and flung it heavily upon the ground again.

'At this time of the rolling year,' the spectre said, 'I suffer most. Why did I walk through crowds of fellow-beings with my eyes turned down, and never raise them to that blessed Star which led the Wise Men to a poor abode? Were there no poor homes to which its light would have conducted *me*?'

Scrooge was very much dismayed to hear the specture going on at this rate, and began to quake exceedingly.

'Hear me!' cried the Ghost. 'My time is nearly gone.'

'I will,' said Scrooge. 'But don't be hard upon me! Don't be flowery, Jacob! Pray!'

'How it is that I appear before you in a shape that you can see, I may not tell. I have sat invisible beside you many and many a day.'

It was not an agreeable idea. Scrooge shivered, and wiped the perspiration from his brow.

'I am here tonight to warn you,' pursued the Ghost, 'that you have yet a chance and hope of escaping my fate. A chance and hope of my procuring, Ebenezer.'

'You were always a good friend to me,' said Scrooge. 'Thank'ee!'

'You will be haunted,' resumed the Ghost, 'by Three Spirits.'

Scrooge's countenance fell almost as low as the Ghost's had done.

'Is that the chance and hope you mentioned, Jacob?' he demanded, in a faltering voice.

'It is.'

'I – I think I'd rather not,' said Scrooge.

'Without their visits,' said the Ghost, 'you cannot hope to shun the path I

tread. Expect the first tomorrow, when the bell tolls one.'

'Couldn't I take 'em all at once, and have it over, Jacob?' hinted Scrooge.

'Expect the second on the next night at the same hour. The third upon the next night when the last stroke of twelve has ceased to vibrate. Look to see me no more; and look that, for your own sake, you remember what has passed between us!'

When it had said these words, the spectre took its wrapper from the table, and bound it round its head, as before. Scrooge knew this by the smart sound its teeth made, when the jaws were brought together by the bandage. He ventured to raise his eyes again, and found his supernatural visitor confronting him in an erect attitude, with its chain wound over and about its arm.

The apparition walked backward from him; and at every step it took, the window raised itself a little, so that when the spectre reached it, it was wide open. It beckoned Scrooge to approach, which he did. When they were within two paces of each other, Marley's Ghost held up its hand, warning him to come no nearer. Scrooge stopped.

Not so much in obedience, as in surprise and fear: for on the raising of the hand, he became sensible of confused noises in the air: incoherent sounds of lamentation and regret; wailings inexpressibly sorrowful and self-accusatory. The spectre, after listening for a moment, joined in the mournful dirge; and floated out upon the bleak, dark night.

Scrooge followed to the window, desperate in his curiosity. He looked out.

The air was filled with phantoms, wandering hither and thither in restless haste, and moaning as they went. Every one of them wore chains like Marley's Ghost. Many had been personally known to Scrooge in their lives. He had been quite familiar with one old ghost, in a white waistcoat, with a monstrous iron safe attached to its ankle, who cried piteously at being unable to assist a wretched woman with an infant, whom it saw below, upon a door-step. The misery with them all was, clearly, that they sought to interfere, for good, in human matters, and had lost the power for ever.

Whether these creatures faded into mist, or mist enshrouded them, he could not tell. But they and their spirit voices faded together; and the night became as it had been when he walked home.

Scrooge closed the window, and examined the door by which the Ghost had entered. It was double-locked, as he had locked it with his own hands, and the bolts were undisturbed. He tried to say 'Humbug!' but stopped at the first syllable. And being, from the emotion he had undergone, much in need of repose, went straight to bed, without undressing, and fell asleep upon the instant.

ONE OF DICKENS'S DAUGHTERS used to tell a story of being in a room with her father when she was small. She was astonished, and even rather frightened, to see Dickens, again and again, rise from his desk, cross to a mirror, try out all manner of faces in it, and return to his desk, from which, from time to time, extraordinary voices were heard. He was trying out his dialogue, just as, in the mirror, he'd been putting on one expression after another so he could describe them. He didn't so much write his books as *live* them, and seemed almost to become the people he was writing about. When in 1846 he wrote his sixth novel, *Dombey and Son*, he said it seemed to him more real than the real world itself.

He hadn't written a novel for three years – a long gap for him. He'd only been planning and editing and contributing to a new national newspaper, acting with his amateur dramatic company, writing two more of his Christmas books, living in Italy, and writing a book about doing that; and now he was living in Switzerland. *Dombey and Son*, he said, was to be a book about pride. It is Mr Dombey, head of a shipping house, who is proud: a rich, cold-hearted man. He has a daughter, Florence, whose nature is as warm as his is not, but he longs for a son. This longing is realized, but his wife dies giving birth to a strange, delicate child, Paul. All of Dombey's attention and care are given to the boy: Florence means very little to him. A foster-mother is chosen to care for Paul. Her name is

Polly Toodle, but the haughty Mr Dombey doesn't want anything to do with real people, so he renames her Mrs Richards, and tells her she is not to become attached to Paul, and he is not to become attached to her. When a foster-mother is no longer needed, she is to go away and forget him, and he is to forget her.

Polly has a son called Biler, which is the way the Toodles pronounce Boiler, a name given to him because steam engines have played an important part in the working life of his father, Mr Toodle. To Biler's dismay, Mr Dombey has found a place for him in a school set up by the Charitable Grinders, the worst of it being that every boy has to wear a uniform: a baize tailed coat and cap, turned up with orange-coloured binding, red stockings, and leather knee-breeches.

One day Polly sets out on an errand taking Paul with her, and they're accompanied by Susan Nipper, a black-eyed fourteen-year-old who looks after Florence, so Florence is with them too. It strikes them on their way home that they might be able to meet Biler coming out of school.

DOMBEY AND SON

Now, it happened that poor Biler's life had been, since yesterday morning, rendered weary by the costume of the Charitable Grinders. The youth of the streets could not endure it. No young vagabond could be brought to bear its contemplation for a moment, without throwing himself upon the unoffending wearer, and doing him a mischief. He had been stoned in the streets. He had been overthrown into gutters; bespattered with mud; violently flattened against posts. Entire strangers to his person had lifted his yellow cap off his head and cast it to the winds. His legs had been handled and pinched. That very morning, he had received a perfectly unsolicited black eye on his way to the Grinders' establishment, and had been punished for it by the master: a superannuated old Grinder of savage disposition, who had been appointed schoolmaster because he didn't know anything, and wasn't fit for anything, and for whose cruel cane all chubby little boys had a perfect fascination.

Thus it fell out that Biler, on his way home, slunk along by narrow passages and back streets, to avoid his tormentors. Being compelled to emerge into the main road, his ill fortune brought him at last where a small party of boys, headed by a ferocious young butcher, were lying in wait for any means of pleasurable excitement that might happen. These, finding a Charitable Grinder in the midst of them, set up a general yell and rushed upon him.

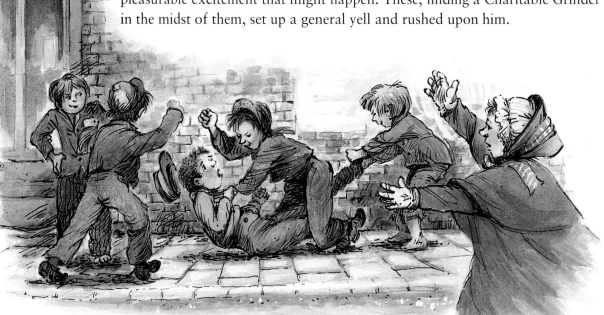

But it so fell out likewise that, at the same time, Polly, looking hopelessly along the road before her, after a good hour's walk, had said it was no use going any further, when suddenly she saw this sight. She no sooner saw it than, uttering a hasty exclamation, and giving Master Dombey to the black-eyed Susan, she started to the rescue of her unhappy little son.

Surprises, like misfortunes, rarely come alone. The astonished Susan Nipper and her two young charges were rescued by the bystanders from under the very wheels of a passing carriage before they knew what had happened; and at that moment (it was market day) a thundering alarm of 'Mad Bull' was raised.

With a wild confusion before her, of people running up and down, and shouting, and wheels running over them, and boys fighting, and mad bulls coming up, and the nurse in the midst of all these dangers being torn to pieces, Florence screamed and ran. She ran till she was exhausted, urging Susan to do the same; and then, stopping and wringing her hands as she remembered they had left the other nurse behind, found, with a sensation of terror not to be described, that she was quite alone.

'Susan! Susan!' cried Florence, clapping her hands in the very ecstasy of her alarm. 'Oh, where are they? Where are they?'

'Where are they?' said an old woman, coming hobbling across as fast as she could from the opposite side of the way. 'Why did you run away from 'em?'

'I was frightened,' answered Florence. 'I didn't know what I did. I thought they were with me. Where are they?'

The old woman took her by the wrist, and said, 'I'll show you.'

She was a very ugly old woman, with red rims round her eyes, and a mouth that mumbled and chattered of itself when she was not speaking. She was miserably dressed, and carried some skins over her arm. She seemed to have followed Florence some little way at all events, for she had lost her breath; and this made her uglier still, as she stood trying to regain it: working her shrivelled yellow face and throat into all sorts of contortions.

Florence was afraid of her, and looked, hesitating, up the street, of which she had almost reached the bottom. It was a solitary place – more a back road than a street – and there was no one in it but herself and the old woman.

'You needn't be frightened now,' said the old woman, still holding her tight. 'Come along with me.'

'I – I don't know you. What's your name?' asked Florence.

'Mrs Brown,' said the old woman. 'Good Mrs Brown.'

'Are they near here?' asked Florence, beginning to be led away.

'Susan ain't far off,' said Good Mrs Brown; 'and the others are close to her.'

'Is anybody hurt?' cried Florence.

'Not a bit of it,' said Good Mrs Brown.

The child shed tears of delight on hearing this, and accompanied the old woman willingly; though she could not help glancing at her face as they went along, and wondering whether Bad Mrs Brown, if there were such a person, was at all like her.

They had not gone far when the old woman turned down a dirty lane, where the mud lay in deep black ruts in the middle of the road. She stopped before a shabby little house, as closely shut up as a house that was full of cracks and crevices could be. Opening the door with a key she took out of her bonnet, she pushed the child before her into a back room, where there was a great heap of rags of different colours lying on the floor; a heap of bones, and a heap of sifted dust or cinders; but there was no furniture at all, and the walls and ceiling were quite black.

The child became so terrified that she was stricken speechless, and looked as though about to swoon.

'Now don't be a young mule,' said Good Mrs Brown, reviving her with a shake. 'I'm not a going to hurt you. Sit upon the rags.'

Florence obeyed her, holding out her folded hands, in mute supplication.

'I'm not a going to keep you, even, above an hour,' said Mrs Brown. 'D'ye understand what I say?'

The child answered with great difficulty, 'Yes.'

'Then,' said Good Mrs Brown, taking her own seat on the bones, 'don't vex me. If you don't, I tell you I won't hurt you. But if you do, I'll kill you. I could have you killed at any time – even if you was in your own bed at home. Now let's know who you are, and what you are, and all about it.'

The old woman's threats and promises, and the dread of giving her offence, enabled Florence to do this bidding, and to tell her little history, or what she knew of it. Mrs Brown listened attentively, until she had finished.

'So your name's Dombey, eh?' said Mrs Brown.

'Yes, ma'am.'

'I want that pretty frock, Miss Dombey,' said Good Mrs Brown, 'and that little bonnet, and a petticoat or two, and anything else you can spare. Come! Take 'em off!'

Florence obeyed, as fast as her trembling hands would allow, keeping, all the while, a frightened eye on Mrs Brown. When she had divested herself of all the articles of apparel mentioned by the lady, Mrs B. examined them at leisure, and seemed tolerably well satisfied with their quality and value.

'Humph!' she said, running her eyes over the child's slight figure. 'I don't see anything

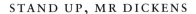
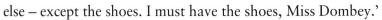

else – except the shoes. I must have the shoes, Miss Dombey.'

Poor little Florence took them off with equal alacrity, only too glad to have any more means of conciliation about her. The old woman then produced some wretched substitutes from the bottom of the heap of rags, which she turned up for that purpose; together with a girl's cloak, quite worn out and very old; and the crushed remains of a bonnet that had probably been picked up from some ditch or dunghill. In this dainty raiment, she instructed Florence to dress herself; and as such preparation seemed a prelude to her release, the child complied with increased readiness, if possible.

In hurriedly putting on the bonnet, if that may be called a bonnet which was more like a pad to carry loads on, she caught it in her hair which grew luxuriantly, and could not immediately disentangle it. Good Mrs Brown whipped out a large pair of scissors, and fell into an unaccountable state of excitement.

'Why couldn't you let me be,' said Mrs Brown, 'when I was contented? You little fool!'

'I beg your pardon. I don't know what I have done,' panted Florence. 'I couldn't help it.'

'Couldn't help it!' cried Mrs Brown. 'How do you expect I can help it? Why, Lord,' said the old woman, 'anybody but me would have had those curls off first of all!'

Florence was so relieved to find that it was only her hair and not her head which Mrs Brown coveted that she offered no resistance or entreaty, and merely raised her mild eyes towards the face of that good soul.

'If I hadn't once had a gal of my own – beyond seas now – that was proud of her hair,' said Mrs Brown, 'I'd have had every lock of it. She's far away, she's far away! Oho! Oho!'

Mrs Brown's was not a melodious cry, but, accompanied with a wild tossing up of her lean arms, it was full of passionate grief, and thrilled to the heart of Florence, whom it frightened more than ever. It had its part, perhaps, in saving her curls; for Mrs Brown, after hovering about her with the scissors for some moments, like a new kind of butterfly, bade her hide them under the bonnet and let no trace of them escape to tempt her. Having accomplished this victory over

herself, Mrs Brown resumed her seat on the bones, and smoked a very short black pipe, mumbling all the time, as if she were eating the stem.

When the pipe was smoked out, she gave the child a rabbit-skin to carry, that she might appear the more like her ordinary companion, and told her that she was now going to lead her to a public street whence she could inquire her way to her friends. But she cautioned her, with threats of deadly vengeance in case of disobedience, not to talk to strangers, nor to repair to her own home (which may have been too near for Mrs Brown's convenience), but to her father's office in the City; also to wait at the street corner where she would be left, until the clock struck three. These directions Mrs Brown enforced with assurances that there would be eyes and ears that would know everything she did; and these directions Florence promised faithfully to observe.

At length, Mrs Brown conducted her changed and ragged little friend through a labyrinth of narrow streets and lanes and alleys, which emerged, after a long time, upon a stable yard, with a gateway at the end, whence the roar of a great thoroughfare made itself audible. Pointing out this gateway, and informing Florence that when the clocks struck three she was to go to the left, Mrs Brown, after making a parting grasp at her hair which seemed involuntary and quite beyond her own control, told her she knew what to do, and bade her go and do it: remembering that she was watched.

With a lighter heart, but still sore afraid, Florence felt herself released, and tripped off to the corner. When she reached it, she looked back and saw the head of Good Mrs Brown peeping out of the low wooden passage, where she had issued her parting injunctions; likewise the fist of Good Mrs Brown shaking towards her. But though she often looked back afterwards – every minute, at least, in her nervous recollection of the old woman – she could not see her again.

Florence remained there, looking at the bustle in the street, and more and more bewildered by it; and in the meanwhile the clocks appeared to have made up their minds never to strike three any more. At last the steeples rang out three o'clock; there was one close by, so she couldn't be mistaken; and – after often looking over her shoulder, and often going a little way, and as often coming back again, lest the all-powerful spies of Mrs Brown should take offence – she hurried off, as fast as she could in her slipshod shoes, holding the rabbit-skin tight in her hand.

All she knew of her father's offices was that they belonged to Dombey and Son, and that was a great power belonging to the City. So she could only ask the way to Dombey and Son's in the City; and as she generally made inquiry of children – being afraid to ask grown people – she got very little satisfaction indeed. But by dint of asking her way to the City after a while, and dropping the rest of her inquiry for the present, she really did advance, by slow degrees, towards the heart of that great region which is governed by the terrible Lord Mayor.

Tired of walking, pushed about, stunned by the noise and confusion, anxious for her brother and the nurses, terrified by what she had undergone; perplexed and frightened alike by what had passed, and what was passing, and what was yet before her; Florence went upon her weary way with tearful eyes, and once or twice could not help stopping to ease her bursting heart by crying bitterly.

It was full two hours later in the afternoon than when she had started on this strange adventure, when, escaping from the clash and clangour of a narrow street full of carts and wagons, she peeped into a kind of wharf or landing-place upon the river-side, where there were a great many packages, casks, and boxes strewn about; a large pair of wooden scales; and a little wooden house on wheels, outside of which, looking at the neighbouring masts and boats, a stout man stood whistling, with his pen behind his ear, and his hands in his pockets, as if his day's work were nearly done.

'Now then!' said this man, happening to turn round. 'We haven't got anything for you, little girl. Be off!'

'If you please, is this the City?' asked the trembling daughter of the Dombeys.

'Ah! It's the City. You know that well enough, I dare say. Be off! We haven't got anything for you.'

'I don't want anything, thank you,' was the timid answer. 'Except to know the way to Dombey and Son's.'

The man, who had been strolling carelessly towards her, seemed surprised by this reply, and looking attentively in her face, rejoined:

'Why, what can *you* want with Dombey and Son's?'

'To know the way there, if you please.'

The man looked at her more curiously, and rubbed the back of his head so hard in his wonderment that he knocked his own hat off.

'Joe!' he called to another man – a labourer – as he picked it up and put it on again.

'Joe it is!' said Joe.

'Where's that young spark of Dombey's who's been watching the shipment of them goods?'

'Just gone, by t'other gate,' said Joe.

'Call him back a minute.'

Joe ran up an archway, bawling as he went, and very soon returned with a blithe-looking boy.

'You work for Dombey, don't you?' said the first man.

'I'm in Dombey's House, Mr Clark,' returned the boy.

'Look'ye here, then,' said Mr Clark.

Following the indication of Mr Clark's hand, the boy approached towards Florence, wondering, as well as he might, what he had to do with her. But she, who had heard what had passed and felt reassured beyond all measure by his lively youthful face and manner, ran eagerly up to him, leaving one of the slipshod shoes upon the ground, and caught his hand in both of hers.

'I am lost, if you please!' said Florence.

'Lost!' cried the boy.

'Yes, I was lost this morning, a long way from here – and I have had my clothes taken away, since – and I am not dressed in my own now – and my name is Florence Dombey, my little brother's only sister – and, oh dear, dear, take care of me, if you please!' sobbed Florence, bursting into tears. At the same time her miserable bonnet falling off, her hair came tumbling down about her face: moving to speechless admiration young Walter Gay, who indeed worked for Dombey's.

Mr Clark stood rapt in amazement: observing under his breath, *I never saw such a start on this wharf before.* Walter picked up the shoe, and put it on the little foot as the Prince in the story might have fitted Cinderella's slipper on. He hung the rabbit-skin over his left arm; gave the right to Florence; and felt like Saint George of England, with the dragon lying dead before him.

'Don't cry, Miss Dombey,' said Walter. 'What a wonderful thing for me that I am here! You are as safe now as if you were guarded by a whole boat's crew of picked men from a man-of-war. Oh, don't cry.'

'I won't cry any more,' said Florence. 'I am only crying for joy.'

'Crying for joy,' thought Walter, 'and I'm the cause of it! Come along, Miss Dombey. There's the other shoe off now! Take mine, Miss Dombey.'

'No, no, no,' said Florence, checking him in the act of impetuously pulling off his own. 'These do better. These do very well.'

'Why, to be sure,' said Walter, glancing at her foot, 'mine are a mile too large. What am I thinking about! You never could walk in *mine*! Come along, Miss Dombey. Let me see the villain who will dare molest you now.'

So Walter, looking immensely fierce, led off Florence, looking very happy; and they went arm-in-arm along the streets, perfectly indifferent to any astonishment that their appearance might or did excite by the way.

T HE YEAR AFTER THE publication of *Dombey*, Dickens set out to write his autobiography: a book that should not be about invented characters, but about Dickens himself, and the facts of his life. But at some point he decided that was wrong for him. He knew a better way of telling the story of his life: to tell of the adventures and misadventures of . . . what name should he use? He settled at last on David Copperfield. (When a friend pointed out that David Copperfield's initials, DC, were the reverse of his own, CD, he was astonished.) In telling the story of this imaginary character he tells, more wonderfully than in any autobiography, an immense amount of his own story. Not the straightforward facts of it: some of David Copperfield's experiences were very close to those of Dickens, some quite unlike his. Copperfield was born in Suffolk, his father already dead; Dickens was born in Chatham, his father very much alive. But the tale of DC is, in much of the detail and in a great deal of the feeling, the tale of CD.

There had been a part of his life that was so painful to him that for a long time he kept it secret. It was what had happened when he was twelve years old. His father was useless at managing his own affairs, and spent more money than he ever had. (An example of the way Dickens used the facts of his life in the novel, but transformed them: there is a character called Micawber, always in trouble over money, who makes the sad observation that to have an annual income of one pound and to spend sixpence less is to be happy; to have an

annual income of one pound and to spend sixpence more is misery.) Charles, the brightest of boys, clever and ambitious, full of imagination and high spirits, was doing well at school when his world fell to pieces: his father was arrested for debt and committed to prison. The boy was taken away from school and sent to work in a factory, sticking labels on bottles of blacking. This factory was just off

the Strand, in London, and for years afterwards, even when he had the habit of walking all over London thinking out the next step in a novel, he couldn't bring himself to go near that corner of the city. The horror of it lasted only six months, but to him it was *absolute* horror. The boys he worked alongside were rough, and had had no schooling at all. Dickens had a great feeling for London roughness. No one has ever written with more sympathy and delight about the vivid coarseness of the poor people who made up so much of London's population in the nineteenth century. But it was a deep shock to him to feel that his hopes in life had suddenly become no better than theirs.

Then his father was released from prison, and Dickens went back to school; but those six months left a scar. Successful and famous as he became, he never felt perfectly safe again. Someone has said that everything he wrote is full of the terror that in a moment you could be switched from huge happiness to huge despair. And that switch – and back again, from despair to happiness – is at the heart of the novel Dickens called *David Copperfield*.

David's father has been six months dead when David is born. An eccentric aunt of his father's, Miss Betsey Trotwood, arrives on the eve of his birth, certain that the child will be a girl, to be named after her. When David's mother turns out to have given birth to a boy, Aunt Betsey aims a blow at the doctor with her bonnet and leaves the house, never to return. David grows up happily with his mother, who is pretty and loving but hasn't a strong character, and their much-loved servant, Peggotty. Peggotty takes him on a marvellous visit, which will have many consequences, to Yarmouth, where her family lives in an upturned boat on the beach; and when they return home, David discovers his mother has married Mr Murdstone, a man with a dark, cruel nature, who now rules the house, together with his disagreeable and cold-hearted sister. David is sent away to school – but his mother dies. He returns home and is neglected, and then is taken to London by Mr Murdstone and finds himself doomed to work in a warehouse at the Thames waterside. There he is set to washing and labelling and corking bottles and packing them into casks. The misery of this existence is so great that one day he resolves to risk everything on an appeal to

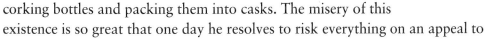

that long-lost aunt of his, Betsey Trotwood. He knows only that she lives at Dover, and so – possessed of three-half pence, a sum so small there's no equivalent for it in our modern currency – he takes on foot to the Dover Road.

After three days, stiff and sore, he decides he can hope to complete his journey only if he manages to sell his jacket, so he looks for a second-hand-clothes shop.

DAVID COPPERFIELD

A T LAST I FOUND one that I thought looked promising, at the corner of a dirty lane, ending in an enclosure full of stinging-nettles, against the palings of which some second-hand sailors' clothes, that seemed to have overflowed the shop, were fluttering among some cots, and rusty guns, and oilskin hats, and certain trays full of so many old rusty keys of so many sizes that they seemed various enough to open all the doors in the world.

Into this shop, which was low and small, and which was darkened rather than lighted by a little window, overhung with clothes, and was descended into by some steps, I went with a palpitating heart; which was not relieved when an ugly old man, with the lower part of his face all covered with a stubbly grey beard, rushed out of a dirty den behind it, and seized me by the hair of my head.

He was a dreadful old man to look at, in a filthy flannel waistcoat, and smelling terribly of rum. His bedstead, covered with a tumbled and ragged piece of patchwork, was in the den he had come from, where another little window showed a prospect of more stinging-nettles, and a lame donkey.

'Oh, what do you want?' grinned this old man, in a fierce whine. 'Oh, my eyes and limbs, what do you want? Oh, my lungs and liver, what do you want? Oh, goroo, goroo!'

I was so much dismayed by these words, and particularly by the repetition of the last unknown one, which was a kind of rattle in his throat, that I could make no answer; whereupon the old man, still holding me by the hair, repeated:

'Oh, what do you want? Oh, my eyes and limbs, what do you want? Oh, my lungs and liver, what do you want? Oh, goroo!' – which he screwed out of himself, with an energy that made his eyes start in his head.

'I wanted to know,' I said, trembling, 'if you would buy a jacket.'

'Oh, let's see the jacket!' cried the old man. 'Oh, my heart on fire, show the jacket to us! Oh, my eyes and limbs, bring the jacket out!'

With that he took his trembling hands, which were like the claws of a great bird, out of my hair; and put on a pair of spectacles.

'Oh, how much for the jacket?' cried the old man, after examining it. 'Oh – goroo! – how much for the jacket?'

'Half a crown,' I answered, recovering myself.

'Oh, my lungs and liver,' cried the old man, 'no! Oh, my eyes, no! Oh, my limbs, no! Eighteen pence. Goroo!'

'Well,' said I, glad to have closed the bargain, 'I'll take eighteen pence.'

'Oh, my liver!' cried the old man, throwing the jacket on a shelf. 'Get out of the shop! Oh, my lungs, get out of the shop! Oh, my eyes and limbs – goroo! – don't ask for money; make it an exchange.'

I never was so frightened in my life, before or since; but I told him humbly that I wanted the money, and that nothing else was of any use to me, but that I would wait for it, as he desired, outside, and had no wish to hurry him. So I went outside, and sat down in the shade in a corner. And I sat there so many hours that the shade became sunlight, and the sunlight became shade again, and still I sat there waiting for the money.

There never was such another drunken madman in that line of business, I hope. That he was well known in the neighbourhood, and enjoyed the reputation of having sold himself to the devil, I soon understood from the visits he received from the boys, who continually came skirmishing about the shop, shouting that legend, and calling to him to bring out his gold. 'You ain't poor, you know, Charley, as you pretend. Bring out your gold. Bring out some of the gold you sold yourself to the devil for. Come! It's in the lining of the mattress, Charley. Rip it open and let's have some!' This, and many offers to lend him a knife for the purpose, exasperated him to such a degree that the whole day was a succession of rushes on his part, and flights on the part of the boys. Sometimes in his rage he would take me for one of them, and come at me, mouthing as if he were going to tear me in pieces; then, remembering me, just in time, would dive into the shop, and lie upon his bed, as I thought from the sound of his voice, yelling in a frantic way, to his own windy tune, the Death of Nelson; with an Oh! before every line, and innumerable Goroos interspersed. As if this were not bad enough for me, the boys, connecting me with the establishment, pelted me, and used me very ill all day.

He made many attempts to induce me to consent to an exchange; at one time coming out with a fishing-rod, at another with a fiddle, at another with a cocked hat, at another with a flute. Each time I asked him, with tears in my eyes, for my money or my jacket. At last he began to pay me in halfpence at a time; and was full two hours getting by easy stages to a shilling.

'Oh, my eyes and limbs!' he then cried, peeping hideously out of the shop, after a long pause. 'Will you go for twopence more?'

'I can't,' I said; 'I shall be starved.'

'Oh, my lungs and liver, will you go for threepence?'

'I would go for nothing, if I could,' I said, 'but I want the money badly.'

'Oh, go – roo! Will you go for fourpence?'

I was so faint and weary that I closed with this offer; and taking the money out of his claw, not without trembling, went away more hungry and thirsty than I had ever been, a little before sunset. But at an expense of threepence I soon refreshed myself completely; and, being in better spirits then, limped seven miles upon my road.

David sleeps that night under a haystack, and finds himself next day among the hopfields, in Kent. Here he falls foul of a tinker, who takes by force the handkerchief he is wearing around his neck. This adventure so frightens him that he hides when he sees people coming, and this delays him seriously. But next day he walks through the sunlight to Dover, reached on the sixth day of his flight from London. This is the town where his aunt lives; but *where* in the town does she live?

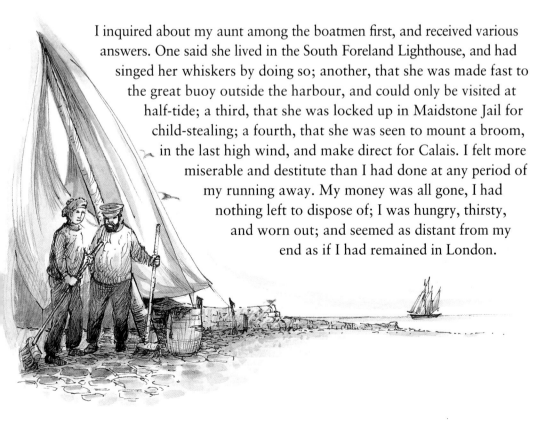

I inquired about my aunt among the boatmen first, and received various answers. One said she lived in the South Foreland Lighthouse, and had singed her whiskers by doing so; another, that she was made fast to the great buoy outside the harbour, and could only be visited at half-tide; a third, that she was locked up in Maidstone Jail for child-stealing; a fourth, that she was seen to mount a broom, in the last high wind, and make direct for Calais. I felt more miserable and destitute than I had done at any period of my running away. My money was all gone, I had nothing left to dispose of; I was hungry, thirsty, and worn out; and seemed as distant from my end as if I had remained in London.

The morning had worn away in these inquiries, and I was sitting on the step of an empty shop at a street corner, near the market-place, when a fly-driver, coming by with his carriage, dropped a horsecloth. Something good-natured in the man's face, as I handed it up, encouraged me to ask him if he could tell me where Miss Trotwood lived; though I had asked the question so often that it almost died upon my lips.

'Trotwood,' said he. 'Let me see. I know the name, too. Old lady?'

'Yes,' I said, 'rather.'

'Pretty stiff in the back?'

'Yes,' I said. 'I should think it very likely.'

'Carries a bag?' said he. 'Bag with a good deal of room in it: is gruffish, and comes down upon you, sharp?'

My heart sank within me as I acknowledged the undoubted accuracy of this description.

'Why then, I tell you what,' said he. 'If you go up there,' pointing with his whip towards the heights, 'and keep right on till you come to some houses facing the sea, I think you'll hear of her. My opinion is, she won't stand anything, so here's a penny for you.'

I accepted the gift thankfully, and bought a loaf with it.

Dispatching this refreshment by the way, I went in the direction my friend had indicated. At length I saw some houses before me; and approaching them, went into a little shop and inquired if they could have the goodness to tell me where Miss Trotwood lived. I addressed the man behind the counter, who was weighing some rice for a young woman; but the latter, taking the inquiry to herself, turned round quickly.

'My mistress?' she said. 'What do you want with her, boy?'

'I want,' I replied, 'to speak to her, if you please.'

'To beg of her, you mean,' retorted the damsel.

'No,' I said, 'indeed.' But suddenly remembering that in truth I came for no other purpose, I felt my face burn.

66

My aunt's handmaid, as I supposed she was from what she had said, put her
rice in a little basket and walked out of the shop, telling me that I could follow
her, if I wanted to know where Miss Trotwood lived. I was by this time in such
a state that my legs shook under me. But I followed the young woman, and we
soon came to a very neat little cottage with cheerful bow-windows; in front of it
was a small square gravelled court or garden full of flowers, carefully tended,
and smelling deliciously.

'This is Miss Trotwood's,' said the young woman. 'Now you know; and that's
all I have got to say.' With which words she hurried into the house, as if to
shake off the responsibility of my appearance; and left me standing at the garden
gate, looking disconsolately over the top of it towards the parlour-window,
where a muslin curtain partly undrawn in the middle, a large round green screen
or fan fastened on to the window-sill, a small table, and a great chair suggested
to me that my aunt might be at that moment seated in awful state.

My shoes were by this time in a woeful condition. The soles had shed
themselves bit by bit, and the upper leathers had broken and burst until the very
shape and form of shoes had departed from them. My hat was so crushed and
bent that no old battered handleless saucepan on a dunghill need have been
ashamed to vie with it. My shirt and trousers, stained with heat, dew, grass, and
the Kentish soil on which I had slept – and torn besides – might have frightened
the birds from my aunt's garden, as I stood at the gate. My hair had known no
comb or brush since I left London. My face, neck, and hands, from
unaccustomed exposure to the air and sun, were burnt to a berry-brown. From
head to foot I was powdered almost as white with chalk and dust. In this plight I
waited to introduce myself to my formidable aunt.

The unbroken stillness of the parlour-window leading me to infer that she was
not there, I lifted up my eyes to the window above it, where I saw a pleasant-
looking gentleman, with a grey head, who shut up one eye in a grotesque
manner, nodded his head at me several times, shook it at me as often, laughed,
and went away.

I was on the point of slinking off, to think how I had best proceed, when there
came out of the house a lady with her handkerchief tied over her cap, and a pair
of gardening gloves on her hands, wearing a gardener's pocket like an apron,

and carrying a great knife. I knew her immediately to be Miss Betsey, for she came stalking out of the house exactly as my poor mother had so often described her stalking up our garden at Blunderstone Rookery.

'Go away!' said Miss Betsey, shaking her head, and making a distant chop in the air with her knife. 'Go along! No boys here!'

I watched her, with my heart at my lips, as she marched to a corner of her garden, and stopped to dig up some little roots there. Then, without a scrap of courage, but with a great deal of desperation, I went softly in and stood beside her, touching her with my finger.

'If you please, ma'am,' I began.

She started and looked up.

'If you please, aunt.'

'EH?' exclaimed Miss Betsey, in a tone of amazement I have never heard approached.

'If you please, aunt, I am your nephew.'

'Oh, Lord!' said my aunt. And sat flat down in the garden path.

'I am David Copperfield, of Blunderstone, in Suffolk – where you came, on the night when I was born, and saw my dear mama. I have been very unhappy since she died. I have been slighted, and taught nothing, and put to work not fit for me. It made me run away to you. I was robbed at first setting out, and have walked all the way, and have never slept in a bed since I began the journey.' Here my self-support gave way all at once; and with a movement of my hands, intended to show her my ragged state, and call it to witness that I had suffered something, I broke into a passion of crying, which I suppose had been pent up within me all the week.

My aunt, with every sort of expression but wonder discharged from her countenance, sat on the gravel, staring at me, until I began to cry; when she got up

in a great hurry, collared me, and took me into the parlour. Her first proceeding there was to unlock a tall press, bring out several bottles, and pour some of the contents of each into my mouth. I think they must have been taken out at random, for I am sure I tasted aniseed water, anchovy sauce, and salad dressing. When she had administered these restoratives, as I was still quite hysterical, and unable to control my sobs, she put me on the sofa, with a shawl under my head, and the handkerchief from her own head under my feet, lest I should sully the cover; and then, sitting herself down behind the green fan or screen I have already mentioned, so that I could not see her face, ejaculated at intervals, 'Mercy on us!' letting those exclamations off like minute guns.

After a time she rang the bell. 'Janet,' said my aunt, when her servant came in. 'Go upstairs, give my compliments to Mr Dick, and say I wish to speak to him.'

Janet looked a little surprised to see me lying stiffly on the sofa (I was afraid to move lest it should be displeasing to my aunt), but went on her errand. My aunt, with her hands behind her, walked up and down the room, until the gentleman who had squinted at me from the upper window came in laughing.

'Mr Dick,' said my aunt, 'don't be a fool, because nobody can be more discreet than you can, when you choose. We all know that. So don't be a fool, whatever you are.'

The gentleman was serious immediately, and looked at me, I thought, as if he would entreat me to say nothing about the window.

'Mr Dick,' said my aunt, 'you have heard me mention David Copperfield? Now don't pretend not to have a memory, because you and I know better.'

'David Copperfield?' said Mr Dick, who did not apear to me to remember much about it. '*David* Copperfield? Oh yes, to be sure. David, certainly.'

'Well,' said my aunt, 'this is his boy, his son. He would be as like his father as it's possible to be, if he was not so like his mother, too.'

'His son?' said Mr Dick. 'David's son? Indeed!'

'Yes,' pursued my aunt, 'and he has done a pretty piece of business. He has run away. Ah! His sister, Betsey Trotwood, never would have run away.' My aunt shook her head firmly, confident in the character of the girl who never was born.

'Oh, you think she wouldn't have run away?' said Mr Dick.

'Bless and save the man,' exclaimed my aunt, sharply, 'how he talks! Don't I know she wouldn't? She would have lived with her god-mother, and we should have been devoted to one another. Where, in the name of wonder, should his sister, Betsey Trotwood, have run from, or to?'

'Nowhere,' said Mr Dick.

'Well then,' returned my aunt, softened by the reply, 'how can you pretend to be wool-gathering, Dick, when you are as sharp as a surgeon's lancet? Now, here you see young David Copperfield, and the question I put to you is, what shall I do with him?'

'What shall you do with him?' said Mr Dick, feebly, scratching his head. 'Oh, do with him?'

'Yes,' said my aunt, with a grave look, and her forefinger held up. 'Come! I want some very sound advice.'

'Why, if I was you,' said Mr Dick, considering, and looking vacantly at me, 'I

71

should – ' the contemplation of me seemed to inspire him with a sudden idea, and he added, briskly, 'I should wash him!'

'Janet,' said my aunt, turning round with a quiet triumph, 'Mr Dick sets us all right. Heat the bath!'

This is not the last piece of good advice given by Mr Dick, who is rather soft in the head: all of which, added together, leads to a new and happier life for David Copperfield. (You can tell this from the titles of the chapters that follow: 'My Aunt Makes Up Her Mind About Me', 'I Make Another Beginning' and 'I am a New Boy in More Senses Than One'.)

In a splendid scene that makes one want to cheer the dreadful Mr Murdstone and his horrid sister, Miss Murdstone, who arrive in Dover to take David back, are sent packing, and David is given a home by his aunt and the wonderfully odd Mr Dick.

But we are still barely a quarter of the way through *The Personal History, Adventures, Experiences and Observations of David Copperfield, of Blunderstone Rookery.*

TWELVE YEARS AND FOUR novels after David Copperfield there were only two and a half novels to come – a half because in the middle of writing the last of them Dickens died. The first of these final books was written for yet another magazine that Dickens had set up. For this new magazine he needed a story that could be told in weekly parts. At the right moment he had what he called 'a very fine grotesque idea.' And out of that idea – he wondered how things might turn out if a poor boy was suddenly and unexpectedly made rich – came *Great Expectations*. The novel ends thrillingly with a pursuit on the river Thames, and to make sure he'd get that right (just as he made sure he got the expressions on faces right by grimacing in a mirror) he hired a Thames steamer for a day and made notes. He finished the novel in Dover: 'I work here like a Steam Engine,' he wrote, 'and walk like Captain Barclay' (the Captain being a famous pedestrian who'd once walked 1,000 hours). One can't help wondering how many thousands of miles Dickens walked during the writing of his fourteen and a half novels.

The hero of *Great Expectations* is Philip Pirrip, known as Pip. He's brought up in a village in marsh country by his sister, who's married to Joe Gargery, the blacksmith. Joe is as kind as Mrs Joe (who uses a cane on Pip that he and Joe call Tickler) is unkind. Pip's mother and father and his five brothers are buried

in the local churchyard, and it's there one raw afternoon towards evening that he has a terrifying encounter with an escaped convict. Under threat of having his heart and liver 'tore out, roasted and ate', he smuggles food to this 'fearful man, with a great iron on his leg'. The man is recaptured and taken back to the prison-ship on the nearby river, but not before he has saved Pip from punishment by claiming it was he who'd stolen the pie and the dram of liquor Pip had taken from Mrs Joe's larder.

One day Mrs Joe brings a puzzling message: a rich lady in town called Miss Havisham wants Pip to come to her large and dismal house and to play there. On his arrival he finds himself face to face with . . .

GREAT EXPECTATIONS

• • • THE STRANGEST LADY I have ever seen, or shall ever see.

She was dressed in rich materials – satins, and lace, and silks – all of white. Her shoes were white. And she had a long white veil dependent from her hair, and she had bridal flowers in her hair, but her hair was white. Some bright jewels sparkled on her neck and on her hands, and some other jewels lay sparkling on the table. Dresses, less splendid than the dress she wore, and half-packed trunks, were scattered about. She had not quite finished dressing, for she had but one shoe on – the other was on the table near her hand – her veil was but half arranged, her watch and chain were put on, and some lace for her bosom lay with those trinkets, and with her handkerchief, and gloves, and some flowers, and a Prayer-book, all confusedly heaped about the looking-glass.

I saw that everything which ought to be white had been white long ago, and was faded and yellow. I saw that the bride within the bridal dress had withered like the dress, and like the flowers, and had no brightness left but the brightness of her sunken eyes. I saw that the dress had been put upon the rounded figure of a young woman, and that the figure upon which it now hung loose had shrunk to skin and bone. Once, I had been taken to see some ghastly waxwork at the Fair, representing I know not what impossible personage lying in state. Once, I had been taken to one of our old marsh churches to see a skeleton in the ashes of a rich dress, that had been dug out of a vault under the church pavement.

Now, waxwork and skeleton seemed to have dark eyes that moved and looked at me. I should have cried out, if I could . . .

With Miss Havisham there's a beautiful but cruelly cold young woman called Estella, who addresses Pip as 'boy'. Miss Havisham makes Estella play cards with Pip (though she says she doesn't want to play with 'a common labouring-boy'). After that he's sent down into the yard where Estella gives him food: 'She put the mug down on the stones, and gave me the bread and meat without looking at me, as insolently as if I were a dog in disgrace.' He's then sent home.

On his second visit Estella is crueller still. She slaps his face and calls him a 'little coarse monster' for saying that she is insulting, and then takes him to Miss Havisham, who sends him into a room opposite the one she's sitting in.

I crossed the staircase landing, and entered the room she indicated. From that room, too, the daylight was completely excluded, and it had an airless smell. A fire had been lately kindled in the damp old-fashioned grate, and it was more disposed to go out than to burn up, and the reluctant smoke which hung in the room seemed colder than the clearer air – like our own marsh mist. Certain wintry branches of candles on the high chimney-piece faintly lighted the chamber. It was spacious, and I dare say had once been handsome, but everything in it was covered with dust and mould, and dropping to pieces. The most prominent object was a long table with a tablecloth spread on it, as if a feast had been in preparation when the house and the clocks all stopped together. A centre-piece of some kind was in the middle of this cloth; it was so heavily overhung with cobwebs that its form was quite undistinguishable; and, as I looked along the yellow expanse out of which I remember its seeming to grow, like a black fungus, I saw speckled-legged spiders with blotchy bodies running home to it, and running out from it, as if some circumstance of the greatest public importance had just transpired in the spider community.

I heard the mice too, rattling behind the panels, as if the same occurrence were important to their interests. But the black beetles took no notice of the agitation, and groped about the hearth in a ponderous elderly way, as if they were short-sighted and hard of hearing, and not on terms with one another.

These crawling things had fascinated my attention, and I was watching them from a distance, when Miss Havisham laid a hand upon my shoulder. In her other hand she had a crutch-headed stick on which she leaned, and she looked like the Witch of the place.

'This,' said she, pointing to the long table with her stick, 'is where I will be laid when I am dead. They shall come and look at me here.'

With some vague misgiving that she might get upon the table then and there and die at once, the complete realization of the ghastly waxwork at the Fair, I shrank under her touch.

'What do you think that is?' she asked me, again pointing with her stick. 'That, where those cobwebs are?'

'I can't guess what it is, ma'am.'

'It's a great cake. A bride-cake. Mine!'

She looked all round the room in a glaring manner, and then said, leaning on me while her hand twitched my shoulder, 'Come, come, come! Walk me, walk me!'

I made out from this that the work I had to do was to walk Miss Havisham round and round the room. Accordingly, I started at once, and she leaned upon my shoulder. She was not physically strong, and after a little time said, 'Slower!' Still, we went at an impatient fitful speed, and as we went, she twitched the hand upon my shoulder, and worked her mouth, and led me to believe that we were going fast because her thoughts went fast. After a while she said, 'Call Estella!' so I went out on the landing and roared that name. Then I returned to Miss Havisham, and we started away again round and round the room.

At last she stopped before the fire, and said, after muttering and looking at it some seconds:

'This is my birthday, Pip.'

I was going to wish her many happy returns, when she lifted her stick.

'I don't suffer it to be spoken of.'

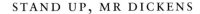

Of course I made no further effort to refer to it.

'On this day of the year, long before you were born, this heap of decay' – stabbing with her crutched stick at the pile of cobwebs on the table but not touching it – 'was brought here. It and I have worn away together. The mice have gnawed at it, and sharper teeth than teeth of mice have gnawed at me.'

She stood looking at the table as if she stood looking at her own figure lying there. I remained quiet. Estella appeared, and she too remained quiet. In the heavy air of the room, and the heavy darkness that brooded in its remoter corners, I even had an alarming fancy that Estella and I might presently begin to decay.

At length Miss Havisham said, 'Let me see you two play at cards; why have you not begun?' With that, we returned to her room, and sat down as before; and again, as before, Miss Havisham watched us all the time.

For her part, Estella treated me as before; except that she did not condescend to speak. When we had played some half-dozen games, a day was appointed for my return, and I was taken down into the yard to be fed in the former dog-like manner. There, too, I was again left to wander about as I liked.

In the garden wall I saw a gate that stood open, and so I strolled into the garden and strolled all over it. It was quite a wildernes, and there were old melon-frames and cucumber-frames in it, which seemed in their decline to have produced a growth of weak attempts at pieces of old hats and boots, with now and then a weedy offshoot into the likeness of a battered saucepan.

When I had exhausted the garden and a greenhouse with nothing in it but a fallen-down grape-vine and some bottles, I found myself in a dismal corner with a window of the house close at hand; and, looking through the window, found myself, to my great surprise, exchanging a broad stare with a pale young gentleman with red eyelids and light hair.

This pale young gentleman quickly disappeared, and reappeared beside me. He had been at his books when I had found myself staring at him, and I now saw that he was inky.

'Halloa,' said he, 'young fellow!'

'Halloa' being a general observation which I had usually observed to be best answered by itself, *I* said 'Halloa!' politely omitting young fellow.

'Who let *you* in?' said he.

'Miss Estella.'

'Come and fight,' said the pale young gentleman.

What could I do but follow him? I have often asked myself the question since: but what else could I do? His manner was so final and I was so astonished that I followed where he led, as if I had been under a spell.

'Stop a minute, though,' he said, wheeling round before we had gone many paces. 'I ought to give you a reason for fighting, too. There it is!' In a most irritating manner he instantly slapped his hands against one another, daintily flung one of his legs up behind him, pulled my hair, slapped his hands again, dipped his head, and butted it into my stomach.

This bull-like proceeding was particularly disagreeable just after bread and meat. I therefore hit out at him, and was going to hit out again, when he said, 'Aha! Would you?' and began dancing backwards and forwards in a manner quite unparalleled within my limited experience.

'Laws of the game!' said he. Here, he skipped from his left leg on to his right. 'Regular rules!' Here, he skipped from his right leg on to his left. 'Come to the ground, and go through the preliminaries!' Here, he dodged backwards and forwards, and did all sorts of things while I looked helplessly at him.

I was secretly afraid of him when I saw him so dexterous; but I felt morally and physically convinced that his light head of hair could have had no business in the pit of my stomach. Therefore, I followed him without a word to a retired nook of the garden, formed by the junction of two walls and screened by some rubbish. On his asking me if I was satisfied with the ground, and on my replying Yes, he begged my leave to absent himself for a moment, and quickly returned with a bottle of water and a sponge dipped in vinegar. 'Available for both,' he said, placing these against the wall. And then fell to pulling off, not only his jacket and waistcoat, but his shirt too, in a manner at once light-hearted, businesslike, and bloodthirsty.

Although he did not look very healthy, these dreadful preparations quite appalled me. I judged him to be about my own age, but he was much taller, and he had a way of spinning himself about that was full of appearance. For the rest, he was a young gentleman in a grey suit (when not denuded for battle), with his elbows, knees, wrists, and heels considerably in advance of the rest of him as to development.

My heart failed me when I saw him squaring at me and eyeing my anatomy as if he were minutely choosing his bone. I never have been so surprised in my life as I was when I let out the first blow, and saw him lying on his back, looking up at me with a bloody nose and his face exceedingly foreshortened.

But he was on his feet directly, and after sponging himself began squaring again. The second greatest surprise I have ever had in my life was seeing him on his back again, looking up at me out of a black eye.

His spirit inspired me with great respect. He seemed to have no strength, and he never once hit me hard, and he was always knocked down; but he would be up again in a moment, sponging himself or drinking out of the water-bottle, and then came at me with an air and a show that made me believe he really was going to do for me at last. He got heavily bruised, for I am sorry to record that the more I hit him, the harder I hit him; but he came up again and again and again, until at last he got a bad fall with the back of his head against the wall. Even after that crisis in our affairs, he got up and turned round and round confusedly a few times, not knowing where I was; but finally went on his knees to his sponge and threw it up, at the same time panting out, 'That means you have won.'

He seemed so brave and innocent that although I had not proposed the contest, I felt but a gloomy satisfaction in my victory. Indeed, I go so far as to hope that I regarded myself, while dressing, as a species of savage young wolf, or other wild beast. However, I got dressed, darkly wiping my face at intervals, and I said, 'Can I help you?' and he said, 'No thankee'; and I said, 'Good afternoon', and *he* said, 'Same to you.'

When I got into the courtyard, I found Estella waiting with the keys. She neither asked me where I had been, nor why I had kept her waiting; and there was a bright flush upon her face, as though something had happened to delight her. Instead of going straight to the gate, too, she stepped back into the passage, and beckoned me.

'Come here! You may kiss me if you like.'

I kissed her cheek as she turned it to me. I think I would have gone through a great deal to kiss her cheek. But I felt that the kiss was given to the coarse common boy as a piece of money might have been, and that it was worth nothing.

What with the cards, and what with the fight, my stay had lasted so long that when I neared home the light on the spit of sand off the point on the marshes was gleaming against a black night-sky, and Joe's furnace was flinging a path of fire across the road.

AFTER *Great Expectations*, Dickens completed one more novel. He went on with his readings, which remained enormously popular. One thing he didn't like was members of the audience following readings in their own copies of his books. That was because he changed things as he went along; he was always ready to do that, as a new joke occurred to him, or he felt the need to make a passage last longer, or come to a quicker end. He had the need for *that* – a quicker end – quite urgently in mind one night when one of the gas jets used to throw that intense light on the reader had been put in the wrong place, and was obviously going to burn through a wire holding a reflector that increased the light. With one eye on the wire, he shortened what he was reading and left the stage in the nick of time. They were able to turn the gas off before the wire was quite burnt through, but nobody in the audience knew of the danger. It was not in Dickens's nature to interrupt his reading even when he was at risk of being struck by several metres of falling metal.

He went on a last reading tour of America. The queues for tickets stretched down whole streets, and round buildings and then round them again; and when he travelled by train, the other passengers stood and cheered him. He treasured the words of a janitor in one of the hotels he stayed in, who'd been at a reading; being German by birth, he spoke in a sort of half German, half American: 'Mr Digguns, you are gread. There is no ent to you! Bedder and bedder. Wot negst!'

85

When he'd given his last performance, in London, he wanted to destroy the famous reading desk – but his daughter Kate successfully begged him to give it to her. He was in the middle of what would have been his fifteenth novel, *The Mystery of Edwin Drood* (a mystery that remains a mystery for ever, though you can try your own hand at solving it: the half that he completed is printed among his books), when he died, aged fifty-eight. That happened at Gad's Hill Place – a house he'd passed when walking with his father, as a boy, and thought he'd like to live in, without guessing that one day he would do so, and make it one of the most famous houses in England.

And after he died people remembered how he could be heard, on many an afternoon, in the lanes near the house, shouting at the top of his voice: rehearsing for another evening of when Mr Dickens would be standing up . . .